MOVIE FAVORITES

Solos and String Orchestra Arrangements
Correlated with Essential Elements String Method

Arranged by
ELLIOT DEL BORGO

Welcome to Essential Elements Movie Favorites! There are two versions of each selection in this versatile book. The SOLO version appears in the beginning of your book. The STRING ORCHESTRA arrangements of each song follows. The supplemental CD recording or string orchestra PIANO PART may be used as an accompaniment for solo performance. Use these recordings when playing solos for friends and family.

ISBN 978-0-7935-8419-2

HAL•LEONARD®
CORPORATION

7777 W. BLUEMOUND RD. P.O. BOX 13819 MILWAUKEE, WI 53213

00868020
2nd Edition

CHARIOTS OF FIRE

Music by VANGELIS
Arranged by ELLIOT DEL BORGO

VIOLIN
olo

0868020

From the Paramount Motion Picture FORREST GUMP

FORREST GUMP-MAIN TITLE

(Feather Theme)

VIOLIN
Solo

Music by ALAN SILVESTR
Arranged by ELLIOT DEL BORGO

00868020

APOLLO 13

(End Credits)

By JAMES HORNER
Arranged by ELLIOT DEL BORGO

VIOLIN
Solo

From DANCES WITH WOLVES
THE JOHN DUNBAR THEME

VIOLIN
Solo

By JOHN BARRY
Arranged by ELLIOT DEL BORGO

00868020

THEME FROM E.T.
(The Extra-Terrestrial)

Music by JOHN WILLIAMS
Arranged by ELLIOT DEL BORGO

VIOLIN
Solo

From the Universal Motion Picture JURASSIC PARK

THEME FROM "JURASSIC PARK"

VIOLIN
Solo

Composed by JOHN WILLIAMS
Arranged by ELLIOT DEL BORGO

00868020

MCA MUSIC PUBLISHING

THE MAN FROM SNOWY RIVER
(Main Title Theme)

By BRUCE ROWLAND
Arranged by ELLIOT DEL BORGO

VIOLIN
Solo

00868020

From the Paramount Motion Picture MISSION: IMPOSSIBLE

MISSION: IMPOSSIBLE THEME

VIOLIN
Solo

By LALO SCHIFRIN
Arranged by ELLIOT DEL BORGO

From the Paramount Motion Picture RAIDERS OF THE LOST ARK

RAIDERS MARCH

VIOLIN
Solo

Music by JOHN WILLIAMS
Arranged by ELLIOT DEL BORGO

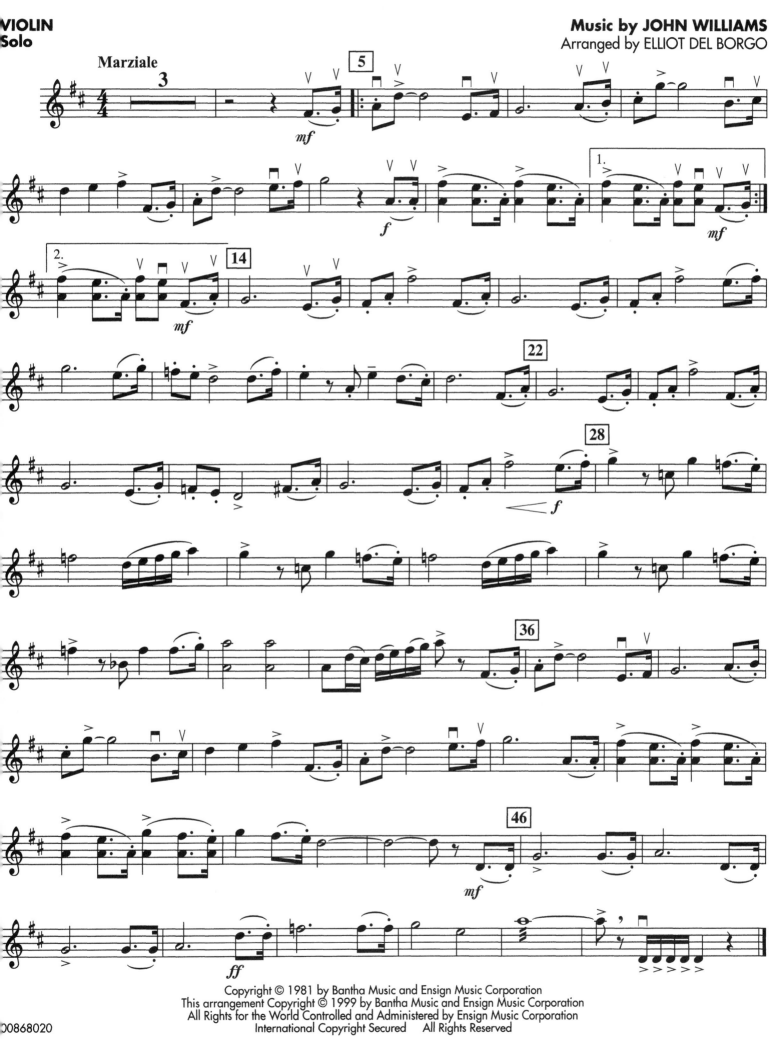

From AN AMERICAN TAIL

SOMEWHERE OUT THERE

VIOLIN
Solo

**Words and Music by JAMES HORNER,
BARRY MANN and CYNTHIA WEIL**
Arranged by ELLIOT DEL BORGO

00868020

MCA MUSIC PUBLISHING

STAR TREK® THE MOTION PICTURE

**VIOLIN
Solo**

Music by JERRY GOLDSMITH
Arranged by ELLIOT DEL BORGO

CHARIOTS OF FIRE

VIOLIN 1
String Orchestra Arrangement

Music by VANGELIS
Arranged by ELLIOT DEL BORGO

00868020

CHARIOTS OF FIRE

VIOLIN 2
String Orchestra Arrangement

Music by VANGELIS
Arranged by ELLIOT DEL BORGO

00868020

From the Paramount Motion Picture FORREST GUMP

FORREST GUMP-MAIN TITLE
(Feather Theme)

VIOLIN 1
String Orchestra Arrangement

Music by ALAN SILVESTRI
Arranged by ELLIOT DEL BORGO

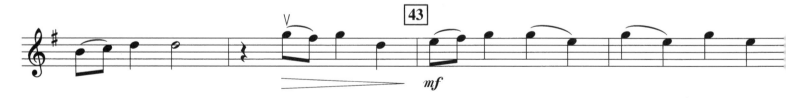

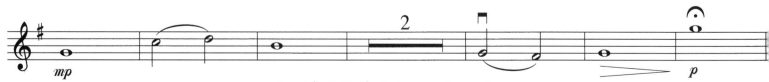

00868020

FORREST GUMP-MAIN TITLE
(Feather Theme)

VIOLIN 2
String Orchestra Arrangement

Music by ALAN SILVESTRI
Arranged by ELLIOT DEL BORGO

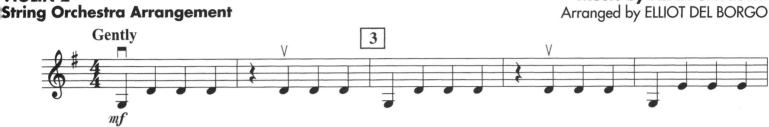

00868020

From **APOLLO 13**
APOLLO 13
(End Credits)

By JAMES HORNER
Arranged by ELLIOT DEL BORGO

VIOLIN 1
String Orchestra Arrangement

MCA MUSIC PUBLISHING

00868020

APOLLO 13

(End Credits)

By JAMES HORNER
Arranged by ELLIOT DEL BORGO

VIOLIN 2
String Orchestra Arrangement

00868020

From DANCES WITH WOLVES

THE JOHN DUNBAR THEME

VIOLIN 1
String Orchestra Arrangement

By JOHN BARRY
Arranged by ELLIOT DEL BORGO

THE JOHN DUNBAR THEME

VIOLIN 2
String Orchestra Arrangement

By JOHN BARRY
Arranged by ELLIOT DEL BORGO

From the Universal Picture E.T. (THE EXTRA-TERRESTRIAL)

THEME FROM E.T.

(The Extra-Terrestrial)

VIOLIN 1
String Orchestra Arrangement

Music by JOHN WILLIAMS
Arranged by ELLIOT DEL BORGO

MCA MUSIC PUBLISHING

THEME FROM E.T.
(The Extra-Terrestrial)

VIOLIN 2
String Orchestra Arrangement

Music by JOHN WILLIAMS
Arranged by ELLIOT DEL BORGO

MCA MUSIC PUBLISHING

00868020

From the Universal Motion Picture JURASSIC PARK

THEME FROM "JURASSIC PARK"

VIOLIN 1
String Orchestra Arrangement

Composed by JOHN WILLIAMS
Arranged by ELLIOT DEL BORGO

00868020

MCA MUSIC PUBLISHING

THEME FROM "JURASSIC PARK"

VIOLIN 2
String Orchestra Arrangement

Composed by JOHN WILLIAMS
Arranged by ELLIOT DEL BORGO

From THE MAN FROM SNOWY RIVER

THE MAN FROM SNOWY RIVER
(Main Title Theme)

By BRUCE ROWLAND
Arranged by ELLIOT DEL BORGO

VIOLIN 1
String Orchestra Arrangement

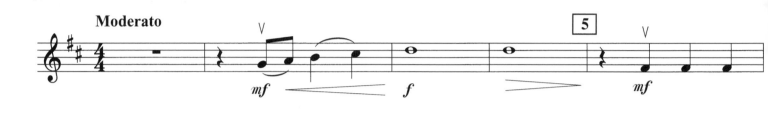

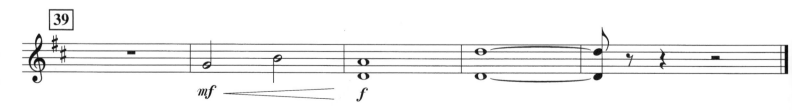

THE MAN FROM SNOWY RIVER

(Main Title Theme)

VIOLIN 2
String Orchestra Arrangement

By BRUCE ROWLAND
Arranged by ELLIOT DEL BORGO

From the Paramount Motion Picture MISSION: IMPOSSIBLE

MISSION: IMPOSSIBLE THEME

VIOLIN 1
String Orchestra Arrangement

By LALO SCHIFRIN
Arranged by ELLIOT DEL BORGO

MISSION: IMPOSSIBLE THEME

VIOLIN 2
String Orchestra Arrangement

By LALO SCHIFRIN
Arranged by ELLIOT DEL BORGO

00868020

From the Paramount Motion Picture RAIDERS OF THE LOST ARK

RAIDERS MARCH

VIOLIN 1
String Orchestra Arrangement

Music by JOHN WILLIAMS
Arranged by ELLIOT DEL BORGO

RAIDERS MARCH

VIOLIN 2
String Orchestra Arrangement

Music by JOHN WILLIAMS
Arranged by ELLIOT DEL BORGO

From AN AMERICAN TAIL

SOMEWHERE OUT THERE

VIOLIN 1
String Orchestra Arrangement

**Words and Music by JAMES HORNER,
BARRY MANN and CYNTHIA WEIL**
Arranged by ELLIOT DEL BORGO

00868020

MCA MUSIC PUBLISHING

From AN AMERICAN TAIL

Somewhere Out There

VIOLIN 2
String Orchestra Arrangement

Words and Music by JAMES HORNER,
BARRY MANN and CYNTHIA WEIL
Arranged by ELLIOT DEL BORGO

MCA MUSIC PUBLISHING

00868020

STAR TREK® THE MOTION PICTURE

VIOLIN 1
String Orchestra Arrangement

Music by JERRY GOLDSMITH
Arranged by ELLIOT DEL BORGO

STAR TREK® THE MOTION PICTURE

VIOLIN 2
String Orchestra Arrangement

Music by JERRY GOLDSMITH
Arranged by ELLIOT DEL BORGO